LIFE LESSONS for MOTHERS

CINDY FRANCIS
AUTHOR OF *LIFE LESSONS FOR WOMEN*

Newport House

Newport House, Inc.
107 R.R. 620 S.,
Suite 7-A
Austin, TX 78734

Life Lessons for Mothers/ Cindy Francis
First Newport House edition, 1993

Cover design by Gayle Smith
Page design by Linda Wells
Typsetting and editorial assistance by Shai Tsur

Manufactured in the United States of America

ISBN 0-939515-48-2

To My Mother,
Donna Kress

INTRODUCTION

Years ago when I was expecting, I had many long talks with my mother about what she had learned while raising me and my five brothers and sisters. She had done a wonderful job, while having a lot more fun than other mothers I knew. What, I wondered, were her secrets? My mother and I would talk and talk, and after she would go, I'd write down the lessons I had learned.

As a mother, I've followed these simple lessons and added my own, and I've been greatly rewarded for having them to guide and inspire me. The "terrible twos" were- for me- "terrific twos," and all the years since have been the richest of my life.

Following the publication of my first book, *Life Lessons for Women*, many of you wrote to ask me to put together another book especially for mothers. I was delighted, and called the most successful and happy mothers I know to ask if they had any lessons to add. Also, I've looked through lots of books by "experts," and found that the gist of what they had to say could usually be put in a sentence or two.

I'm excited and pleased to present you now with my life lessons for mothers. I hope you'll not only read and enjoy them, but will take them to heart and *live* them. They can bring you lots of joy and love and ease. I know.

LIFE
LESSONS
for MOTHERS

The greatest gift you have to give your children is *you*.

When you talk to your child, mostly listen.

Take care of yourself, so you can take care of others.

Change is inevitable, so welcome it.

Always give in to the
urge to hug your child.

Setting limits is good for
children. They'll complain,
but what they'll feel is *relief*.

You'll never be an "Absolutely Perfect Mother." Be a "Good Enough Mother."

If things don't work out, it's okay to cry- but also *learn*.

Teach your children they're unique. That way, they won't feel pressure to be like everybody else.

Ask your child what she likes most to do with you. Do that more often.

Say "I'm sorry" when you're wrong.

Your child will do as you do, not as you say. So set a good example.

Catch your child
doing things *right*.

Be loving, even when
you don't feel loving.

Forgive yourself for the
mistakes you have made.

Encourage your child
every chance you get.

Be flexible with rules.

Recognize and accept
your child's feelings.

Look for win/win solutions.

Remember that when you tell
your children to act their age,
they probably already are.

Some time each day, give your
child your undivided attention.

Ask for your child's
opinion more often.

If you feel overwhelmed, just
start doing one thing at a time.

Tell your children, "I love
you just the way you are."

Take time out every day to have fun.

Give your children opportunities to make *real* contributions to the family.

Go to the park. *Everybody* plays!

Don't compare your children to others. Value them each for their own gifts.

Life Lessons you can learn from your children:

Play more.

Be curious.

Get all wrapped up in what you're doing.

Even the littlest things can bring you pleasure.

Treat your children the way you wish you had been treated when you were a youngster.

Show your respect by introducing your child by name to everyone who comes over.

Be your child's biggest fan.

Exercise together.

When your child is angry, say out loud,
"I think you need a big hug"- and then
give it!

Having your house look like *House
Beautiful* isn't a good use of time.
Settle for *House Pretty Clean.*

Get up early and watch the sun rise together.

Tell your child, "My life is so much better because *you* are here."

Build an extended family, whether it's made up of relatives or friends.

Plant a tree together.

When there's conflict, focus
on the role *you* play.

To belong is your children's
underlying goal- even when they're
misbehaving. Give them constructive
ways to belong.

Go to a parade.

Spend time together
in the library.

Ask questions that begin with "How,"
"Why," and "Tell me about." These
encourage children to speak up.

Build your children's self-esteem by letting them solve most of their own problems.

Have a special time each week for you and your child to do something together. With a teenager, ask for this time because *you* need it.

Go to a pond and skip stones.

Children will believe what you say.
So be sure what you say builds them up.

Do what *you* feel is right for
your children, regardless of
what "everyone else is doing."

Teach that what other kids
say about them is just their
opinion, not the *truth.*

If you work, don't feel guilty.
Every single study ever done shows
children of working mothers do just
as well as other children.

Be grateful for your family- problems and all.

Have more family picnics.

Go bird watching together.

Nothing happens by itself.
You have to *work* at having
a good family life.

Let your children have their own books.

Give up comparing your family with the *Brady Bunch/ Father Knows Best* images you grew up with. Those were TV fantasies; your family is real.

Bake cookies together from scratch.

Take time to be apart from
your children. It will give you
all a chance to grow.

Given a little training and a
little practice, most children
can far exceed our expectations.

Toast the sunset with
a glass of juice.

Children act up when they feel useless.
Let them help with cooking, gardening,
record-keeping. And when they're older,
help them find jobs.

Praise your child for sharing.

Keep your perspective. Problems "come to pass"- not to stay.

Meet your children's friends. Meet their parents too, and keep in touch with them so you can compare notes.

Compliment more than you criticize.

Teach your children good eating habits when they're young and they'll keep them all their lives.

Have family projects like putting up a birdhouse, planting a garden, and starting a family photo album.

Encouragements kids would benefit from hearing more often:

"Thanks! You really made a difference."
"I couldn't have done it better myself."
"I enjoyed working on that with you."
"You've improved!"
"I have faith in you."

Even if your child isn't good at listening to you, she will certainly be good at imitating you.

Give your children problems like, "How can we cut our electricity bill?" Let them research answers and help with solutions.

Have your children learn first aid.

Let your children know they
can always express themselves
freely to you about everything.

Take a nature hike together.

Have your own outside interests.
Don't live through your children.

Teach your children your
family's history, the struggles
and successes that led to all
of you being where you are.

Talk about values if you expect your child to grow up with values.

Most things that *can* go wrong, don't.

When things *do* go wrong, keep your perspective in describing them. Most aren't "terrible," just "unfortunate."

Keep your promises.

Everybody help recycle newspapers.

Help your child become an expert at *something*, whether it's playing the flute, ballet, karate, or baseball cards.

You'll never get everyone's approval of everything you do as a mother. So don't bother trying.

Tell your children how
proud you are of them.

Let your children know
that if there's trouble, you'll
always be there.

Invite over positive people who
feel good about themselves.

Let your children "overhear" you praising them.

Watch for the evening star together. Make a wish.

Make sure your child understands new rules. Do this by asking her to tell you the rule in her own words.

Have Polynesia night, with
everyone dressed like natives.

Hear your children out, even if
you think your answer will be no.

Make it clear your love doesn't
depend on their performance.

Talk about the life lessons to be
learned from other people's mistakes.

Everyone- not just *you*- can
help out around the house.

Read *Children, The Challenge*
to learn better ways to raise
responsible children.

Make it clear *you* like compliments, too. When you do a good job, say, "Okay, I'm open for compliments!"

It's easy for mothers to become isolated. Spend time with friends. And if you don't have them, *make* them.

*When you need help,
ask for it.*

Have a family movie night, complete with pizza and popcorn.

Be firm where safety is concerned.

If your child has problems with school work, get help right away, before he gets really behind.

Put on an old Chubby Checkers record and twist with your child.

To relate better, sit or kneel down to your child's level.

If your child has an overcrowded schedule, help him cut out something.

If your child wants to talk or play when you're busy, set a time and promise him attention then.

Although you have a powerful connection, your child is separate and has different needs, emotions, and desires. Respect them.

Go bike riding together.

If you've got questions about your child's behavior, ask other mothers.

If you've got serious questions, see a pediatrician or counselor. Ask for help for both your child *and you.*

*Work on problems
while they're small.*

Share with your child
your own life lessons.

Read "The Giving Tree" together.

Balance is the key. Balance work
with play, time with the children
with time alone.

When you listen, focus on
what your child is *feeling*.

Be sure your child gets
familiar with computers.

You are not responsible for everything
going well for everyone all the time.

Ask your children questions
about things *they* are interested in.

For one day, count how many times you
criticize- and praise- your children. Work
at criticizing less and praising more.

Talk problems out.

When you're working around
the house, explain what
you're doing and ask for help.

Plan family activities, so watching
TV isn't the only thing to do.

*Show your children
you're on their side.*

Pause, and take stock of what
really matters to you. Put
your time and energy *there*.

Quality time is important, but
sometimes so is the quantity of time.

Visualize success for yourself
and your children.

Give your children some privacy.

Tell your child what *to* do
instead of what *not* to do.

Take a warm bubble bath
after the kids are in bed.

As your children grow older, the way
you treat them needs to keep pace. Much
teenage rebellion comes from treating
them like they're 10 when they're 15.

Everyone in the family name three things every other person does well.

Read *How to Get Control of Your Time and Your Life* to get organized.

Give your full attention when you talk. Don't read or watch TV.

Teach your children there are better ways than whining and hitting to solve problems.

Instead of ordering your kids to put on sweaters and jackets, let them carry them and put them on if they feel cold.

Tell your children how special they are to you.

Make having fun a priority!

To produce a happy
child, be a happy parent.

Every weekend, explore together
someplace new in your area.

Get involved in your child's education by working positively with the school.

Read *Calvin and Hobbes* together. Ask why the characters act the funny way they do.

Blow up a balloon and play volleyball with it.

Important lesson: *life isn't fair.*

Tell your children, "I love you" each morning before they leave home.

You can teach your children how to clean their rooms, but don't expect too much.

Punish your children by calling "time outs" and by withdrawing privileges.

Solve a puzzle together.

It takes two to make an argument.
Don't be one of them.

Get the *Consumer Reports Buying
Guide* and when you're going
shopping, let your child pick out
the best buy.

Nurture your child- not just with food, but with kind words as well.

Get together with other mothers
and swap stories.

Start a journal to keep track of
what you've learned and the
successes you've had.

Get a book on parenting and look up
what to expect at your child's age.

Have lighthearted "punishments":

Whoever has her elbows on the table must sing a song.

Swear words = 10c

Saying something negative about another family member = 25c

Enjoy the gifts life is presenting
you at this moment.

Never criticize in front of others.

When you're upset, be careful not
to say things you might regret.

Take lots of pictures.

Sometime, when your children expect punishment, give them a big hug instead.

For a laugh, read together the *George and Martha* books, the *Cut-Ups* books, and anything else by James Marshall.

Show your love by being kind.

Growth comes with frustration.
Be a source of support.

Once you have criticized your
child's actions, don't bring it up again.

Tell your child often,
"I love you,
no matter what."

Set reasonable limits.

At bedtime, establish a routine
that winds things down and
gets your child ready for sleep.

Have fruits and vegetables- instead
of candy- for your kids to snack on.

Think how you'd feel in your child's place.

Have a special dinner in honor of your children.

Share memories of when you were your child's age.

When your child gets discouraged, remind her of all the things she couldn't do not long ago- and now can.

At night, sit outside on a blanket and look at the stars.

Hold family meetings to clear up gripes.

Set up a tent in the living room and have dinner in it.

Treat all your children equally.

Have your kids take music lessons.
Let them quit if they don't like it.

Rituals, like having dinner together,
make children feel more secure.

Even if your child fails, praise the effort.

How to communicate when you and your child are mad: One person talks at a time. The listener has to give back the gist of what the talker says to the talker's satisfaction before she gets her turn to speak.

Arguing Do's:

Bring up one problem at a time.

Focus on the problem.

Be specific about your complaints.

Compromise if possible.

Arguing Don'ts:

No yelling or swearing.

No name-calling.

No questioning motives.

No bringing up the past.

Praise-
not just success-
but also improvement.

Lie on the floor and read the encyclopedia together.

Your children provide you with a second chance to do the things you loved as a youngster.
Take that chance.

Cook a meal together, with everybody in charge of one dish.

If you're too busy to have fun with your children, you're too busy.

When you're driving, hand your child a map and ask her to direct you to your destination.

Compliment your children often, and you'll give them a reputation to live *up* to!

Sing songs around a campfire.

Let your children progress at their own speed.

If the discipline you're using isn't working, do something different.

The behavior may be bad,
but never the child.

If you expect your children to be "perfect," you will always be disappointed.

See who can make the funniest face.

Teach that failure is never
final unless you give up.

Once a month, spend a
whole day doing whatever
your child wants to do.

Be happy as your children need
you less and less. That's how
it's *supposed* to be.

Teach that while the "easy way" in
the *short* run is to be lazy and goof
off in school, that often turns out to
be the hard way in the *long* run.

Pause, and notice the beauty around you.

Three steps to take when
children misbehave:

1. Briefly describe the behavior.
2. Tell how you feel about it.
3. Affirm that you know the
   child can do better.

Instead of coaxing your children out of bed every morning, buy them alarm clocks. If they're late, let them have the consequences.

Stay out of your children's fights unless someone is in danger. Let them work things out themselves.

Surprise your child with little gifts.

The best way to get your children
to listen to you is to listen to them.

Let family privileges coincide
with responsibilities.

Never say your child is "shy."
Instead, explain, "She doesn't
want to talk right now."

If your child acts shy, practice with
her in front of a mirror smiling,
making eye contact, and keeping
her legs and arms uncrossed.

Tell your children stories in which *they* are the heroes.

When your kids grow up, they won't remember whether the house was perfectly neat and clean. But they will remember whether or not you spent time with them.

Better to be a model than a critic.

When you get angry, remember it's the result of *your* thinking, not what your child is doing.

Teach that no one is perfect- not you, not them, not anyone. And nothing is perfect. But it's possible to be happy in an imperfect world.

Seek first to understand,
then to be understood.

When your child tells you problems,
show you really understand by
repeating the essence of what you
heard and asking if you're right.

When you're excited,
let it show!

Have talks at bedtime.
Your child will talk more
in order to stay up later.

With teenagers, have
talktime while driving and
while eating pizza.

Fly a kite together.

Send your children off in
the morning with a hug.

A positive word or smile
everyday can propel your
child to success.

Replenish yourself by taking time to be alone.

Help a charity drive together.

The only person you can control is yourself.

Build trust by going on a "blind hike," in which you take turns closing your eyes and being led around the neighborhood.

Encourage your child
to think BIG!

Teach your children the *immediate* bad
consequences of smoking- it makes you
cough and your breath and clothes smell
bad. Children seldom think long-term.

Teach also the *immediate* bad consequences of drinking- it makes it hard for you to think and learn and play. It makes you say and do stupid things you may regret later. And it often makes you have bad accidents

Everyone tape a message to send to someone far away.

Don't do for children what
they can do for themselves.

When your children outgrow
clothes, give them to the poor.

For one day, keep track of all
the sugar your child eats. Put that
amount in a bottle and show it to her.

Report cards are *your child's*- not *yours*.

Let your children see that you have shortcomings and suffer setbacks. This will help them be more realistic about themselves.

Nurture yourself, *too*.

Go to garage sales together.

Help your child plan short-term goals (like going camping) and long-term goals (like going to college).

Let your child have input into solutions for problems, especially those which concern her.

If you can afford it, get help with your housework.

Try to have a sit-down family meal at least three times a week. Turn off all distractions like the TV and stereo.

When your child takes a wrong turn, gently help her get back on track.

Keep instructions simple.

Play with your child every day.

Plan your child's parties around activities like swimming and bowling.

Be consistent.

Attend your child's school activities.

Mark off your child's height on a closet wall. Watch them grow!

You can't *assume* your kids understand their homework. Look it over to see if they need help.

Visualize the outcomes you want.

Put a surprise love note under everybody's plate at dinner.

When you're angry, take five minutes to cool off.

Kids sometimes have to make their own mistakes before they learn from them.

At bedtime, get the conversation going by asking, "What's the best thing that happened to you today? The worst?"

Use the past tense when criticizing.
For example, say "you forgot"
rather than "you always forget."

Let your child take responsibility
for her actions- and for coping
with what follows.

Read your children stories
about successful people.

Be specific with praise.
It'll mean more.

Make a list of everything you have to do
each day. Do the most important first.

Shower your kids with kindness!

Be honest (they'll know if you're not anyway).

Have "Family Night" once a week. Everybody does something fun together.

Follow the rules yourself that you set for your child.